JIǍK° BÀ BEH?
A TASTE OF SINGAPOREAN HOKKIEN

An Introduction to Spoken Singaporean Hokkien

Zara Anjali Child

Disclaimer:

The purpose of this book is to give you an introduction to spoken Singaporean Hokkien in a fun and easy manner. The romanization system used in this book is a modified version of Eugene Lee's romanization system for Singaporean Hokkien. Because of a variety of factors, such as tone sandhi and regional differences, words in this book may be pronounced or romanized differently than what your family or other Hokkien speakers consider correct. This book has been reviewed by native Hokkien speakers. As someone who is still learning Hokkien, I aim simply to document how Hokkien is spoken by these native speakers so that other students of this language who may be struggling to find learning materials can have another resource for their own learning journey.

I alone am responsible for all errors made in this text.

Zara Anjali Child, 2023

This book is dedicated to my *guǎ-gōng* and *guǎ-mà*, and all who want to learn Hokkien but don't know where to start.

TABLE OF CONTENTS

INTRODUCTION

WHY SINGAPOREAN HOKKIEN?

Jiǎk° bà beh? Have you eaten yet? This once common greeting among family and friends in Singapore is now rarely used. Speakers of this Chinese dialect—which some linguists consider a separate language—are now far and few between. Over the past 40 years, English and Mandarin have become the most widely spoken languages in Singapore. Hokkien, once spoken by the majority of Singaporeans, is now mainly spoken by a dwindling number of elderly people.

In 1979, the Prime Minister of Singapore, Lee Kuan Yew, launched the Speak Mandarin Campaign. Seeking to create a common language that could ease communication between Chinese Singaporeans from different dialect groups, the campaign promoted the use of Mandarin Chinese over other Chinese dialects. At that time, Chinese dialects such as Hokkien, Cantonese, and Teochew were the mother tongue of nearly three in four Singaporeans. In contrast, Mandarin was spoken by a mere two percent (Johnson). But Lee considered Mandarin the most strategic choice for the young nation state.

Within two years of the campaign's launch, the government had essentially banned the use of dialects. Radio broadcasts and television shows were aired exclusively in Mandarin or English. Students who spoke dialects were sometimes fined and made to write "I will not speak dialects" hundreds of times (Johnson). So while the campaign may have succeeded in boosting the number of Mandarin speakers, it also isolated a whole generation of Singaporeans. Cut off from society, many of the elderly found their words lost in translation. Communication within families grew more difficult, and large swaths of a rich cultural heritage were lost.

Singapore's case of linguistic repression is far from uncommon, and many languages around the world have become critically endangered for similar reasons. Strochlic estimates that 50 to 90 percent of the world's remaining languages will be lost by the end of the century. Diminishing linguistic diversity is tantamount to the loss of unique culture. Songs, stories, and jokes that formed part of previous generations' cultural identity are lost to future generations.

But all hope is not lost. People are starting to recognize the cost of language loss and to appreciate the importance of languages that are not widely spoken. This shift in perspective helps explain why endangered languages such as Hawaiian and Cornish have developed small but growing communities of speakers. But for those wishing to learn dying Chinese dialects like Hokkien, finding learning materials is a significant challenge. My search for Hokkien language materials, including a trip to Singapore's National Library, turned up empty.

Every two weeks, a language dies with its last speaker, and hundreds are on the brink of extinction (Strochlic). Let's make sure Hokkien isn't one of them.

Sources:

Johnson, Ian. "In Singapore, Chinese Dialects Revive after Decades of Restrictions." The New York Times, 26 Aug. 2017, www.nytimes.com/2017/08/26/world/asia/singapore-language-hokkien-mandarin.html.
Strochlic, Nina. "Saving the World's Dying and Disappearing Languages." Culture, 3 May 2021, www.nationalgeographic.com/culture/article/saving-dying-disappearing-languages-wikitongues-culture.

TIPS FOR LEARNING

There is no one correct path to learning a new language. Although immersion is believed to be the best technique for learning a language quickly, for many language learners, especially those of endangered languages, immersion is not possible. This book is not aimed at getting you to fluency in Singaporean Hokkien. It simply aims to provide an introduction to spoken Singaporean Hokkien. Here are some tips to help you get the most out of this book and to immerse yourself in the language.

- Review the material in this book every day if possible, repeating the words and phrases out loud.
- Try to form your own sentences using the patterns and vocabulary in the chapters.
- Talk to yourself in Hokkien. It does not matter if your Hokkien is broken. What matters is that you try. If you do, you will find your speaking and pronunciation improving.
- Use the online flashcards that I have made available through Quizlet (username savesghokkien)
- Listen to Hokkien music. Spotify, Apple Music, and YouTube are great places to find Hokkien music. In the absence of a Hokkien-speaking community, listening to Hokkien songs is a good way for you to get used to the pronunciation and sound of Hokkien.
- Listen to the LearnDialect.Sg podcasts on Spotify for Hokkien.
- Watch Hokkien shows online.
- For individual or group Hokkien lessons, reach out to LearnDialect.Sg!

No single textbook can make you fluent in a language, and this book is no exception in that regard. I simply hope this book will give you a taste of Singaporean Hokkien. Enjoy!

PRONUNCIATION

Hokkien pronunciation is undeniably hard. Resources to learn Hokkien are so scarce, and there are a variety of systems to romanize the language. The most common system, POJ, is designed for Southern Min languages like Hokkien and Teochew. But, this system is difficult to learn. Another system used to romanize Hokkien, the IPA system, has complex symbols and is very difficult to pick up. My Hokkien teacher, Eugene Lee, found a way to approximate the tones and pronunciations of Hokkien using a modified version of pinyin. Pinyin is the romanization of Mandarin Chinese characters. Since this book is targeted towards those who want to quickly pick up basic spoken Hokkien, this book uses a modified version of Eugene Lee's romanization. Many Singaporeans are already familiar with pinyin, allowing this book to be reached by a wider community. In fact, when I finished the first draft of this book, I tested the pronunciation system by having an English speaker familiar with pinyin read sample sentences from this book out loud to a native Hokkien speaker. The native Hokkien speaker found that around nine out of ten sentences that the English speaker sounded out were correct pronunciation.

TONES

Hokkien is a tonal language. Over time, the tones of Hokkien have changed, merged, and adapted. My Hokkien teacher taught me with a total of five tones. This, in my opinion, is the simplest and most efficient way to learn Hokkien.

The graphic below represents the five tones:

	1st Tone High Flat	2nd Tone Gradual Rise	3rd Tone Drop then Rise	4th Tone Sharp Drop	5th Tone Middle Flat
So	——				
Fa					
me					——
Re					
Do					
Example, Si					
	sī	sí	sǐ	sì	si
	Poem 诗	Time period 时	Four 四	Death 死	Yes 是

The following are descriptions of the five Hokkien tones. Practice saying them out loud a few times.

1st Tone - High Flat
- Speak a bit higher than your normal voice, but don't feel like you have to put a lot of effort into speaking high.
- Words with this tone have a straight line above the vowel (sī).

2nd Tone - Gradual Rise
- Start from a slightly low pitch and end at a pitch slightly above your normal voice.
- Words with this tone have a rising line above the vowel (sí).

3rd Tone - Drop then Rise
- Start at your normal voice, then dip to a lower pitch before ending at a higher pitch.
- Words with this tone have a small v above the vowel (sǐ).

4th Tone - Sharp Drop
- Start slightly higher than your normal voice, then go down quickly and strongly.
- Words with this tone have a a falling line above the vowel (sì).

5th Tone - Middle Flat
- Speak at a middle or low and flat pitch.
- Words with this tone do not have a symbol marking.

Nasal
- Certain Hokkien words have a nasal sound, these will be noted with a dash and an N next to the word (hua-N).

VOWELS

The chart below shows the most common ways to pronounce vowels in Hokkien romanization. However, know that these vowel sounds may not always follow these rules. Hokkien words are pronounced differently in context because of tone sandhi, as well as because of regional differences among speakers of Hokkien.

Vowel	Pronunciation	Hokkien Word	Word Pronunciation
ā	"aah" like a sheep's *baa*	wà (me)	*wah*
ē	"ai" like the ai in *ain't*	seng kū (body)	*saing khu*
ī	"ee" like the letter e	lì (you)	*lee*
ō	"oh" like the letter o	hò (good)	*hoh*
ū	"oo" like the o in *cool*	wǔ (are/have)	*ooo*

CONSONANTS

The consonants in Hokkien are pronounced as they are in English except for the following:

c - This is a "ts" sound. For example, the word for "seven" is *cìt* (ts-ee-t).

p - This sounds like an English "p" but the letter is often aspirated meaning that you should feel a puff of air coming out of your mouth when you say it. An example of this is the word for "friend," *pěng yìu* (peing yiew). Feel the push of air out of your mouth when saying *pěng*.

z - In Hokkien, "z" sounds like a "dz" sound in English. This is also like the "ds" sound in the word "kids." An example of this is the word "early" or *zá* (dzaa).

A few combinations of consonants must be touched on as they can be tricky to pronounce.

kh – Sounds like a "k" sound but air is pushed out of your mouth when saying it.

ng – This is a nasal sound. Try saying "hmm" as if you were debating what to say ("Hmm, I don't know."). Then, keeping that hum going, open your lips and have your tongue touch the spot where you pronounce "ng" (to figure that out, say "sang" and you'll see where your tongue curls up).

dng – Try repeating the previous "ng" sound but add an English "d" sound in front.

If you are having a hard time pronouncing these combinations, do not worry. Pronunciation takesKnow that even among fluent Hokkien speakers in Singapore, Hokkien is pronounced differently. Chances are that you will be understood if the rest of your sentence is correct. Don't focus on being perfect, just keep practicing.

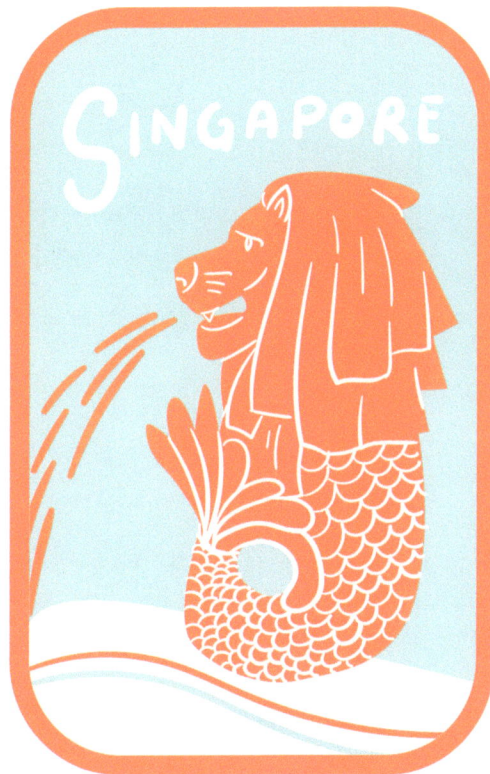

NUMBERS

Hokkien numbers are quite simple. They function similarly to those in Mandarin Chinese.

0	1	2	3	4	5	6	7	8	9	10
kŏng	yĭt°	li	să	sĭ	gor	lằk°	cĭt°	pŏeh°	gào	zàp°

Generally in Hokkien, if a word is the final in a sequence, it keeps its original tone. If it is the first of a sequence, or is placed between two words, the tone of the word will change. This is called tone sandhi. These are the numbers with tone sandhi.

0	1	2	3	4	5	6	7	8	9	10
kòng	yìt°	lĭ	sa	sì	gŏr	lăk°	cit°	pòeh°	gáo	zăp°

For two-digit numbers, place the unit number (like the 2 in 12, or the 5 in 15) after *zăp°*.

11	12	13	14	15	16	17	18	19
zăp° yĭt°	zăp° li	zăp° să	zăp° sĭ	zăp° gor	zăp° lằk°	zăp° cĭt°	zăp° pŏeh°	zăp° gào

For numbers 20 through 90, place the unit number before *zăp°*.

20	30	40	50	60	70	80	90
lĭ zàp°	sa zàp°	sì zàp°	gŏr zàp°	lăk° zàp°	cit° zàp°	pòeh° zàp°	gáo zàp°

Other two-digit numbers are formed by simply adding the unit number to the 20, 30, 40, etc.

25	33	42	51	61	75	81	99
lĭ zàp° gào	sa zăp° să	sì zàp° li	gŏr zàp° yĭt°	lăk° zàp° yĭt°	cit° zàp° gor	pòeh° zàp° li	gáo zăp° gào

Hundreds - "One hundred" in Hokkien is *păh°*. Add the unit number before the *păh°* to say 100, 200, 300, etc.

100	200	300	400	500	600	700	800	900
jĭt° păh°	ňng păh°	sa păh°	sì păh°	gŏr păh°	lăk° păh°	cĭt° păh°	pòeh păh°	gáo păh°

To add to the hundreds, simply say the numbers (like the 25 in 125) after the hundreds. The only exception to this is with number 1-9 after the hundred. You must add "zero" or *kòng* before the number. See the examples below.

105	250	565
jĭt° pàh° kòng gor	ňng pàh° gŏr zàp°	gŏr pàh° lăk° zăp° gor

Thousand in Hokkien is *ceing*. Simply place the unit number before the *ceing*.

1000	2000	3000
jĭt° ceing	ňng ceing	să ceing

INTRODUCTIONS

In this chapter, we will learn the Hokkien pronouns, as well as how to introduce your name, greet others, say your country of origin, and your age.

PRONOUNS

These are the pronouns in Hokkien. They are pretty simple to understand. In order to talk about multiple people, or make a pronoun plural, add *náng*.

I / Me wà	We wà náng
You lì	Y'all lì náng
He / She yi	They yi náng

> (!) **Important note!**
> Some Hokkien speakers use *láng* instead of *náng* to make pronouns plural. It is really a matter of personal preference, and both work. Say whatever you prefer.

WHAT'S YOUR NAME?

In Hokkien, *giò* means "to be called." *Sìh° mìh°* means "what" and *miá* means "name." Put it all together, and *lì giò sìh° mìh° miá* means "what is your name?"

To respond, you can say *wà ěh miá sǐ*, meaning "my name is." The word *ěh* is used to indicate possession.

You can change out the pronouns to introduce other people as well. For example, "what is his/her name" would be *yi giò sìh° mìh° miá* and "his/her name is" would be *yi ěh miá sǐ*.

lì giò sìh° mìh° miá?
(what is your name?)

wà ěh miá sǐ mei!
(my name is mei!)

GREETINGS

Hello - lì hò
- *Lì hò* literally means "you good" in Hokkien.
- *Lì* means "you" and *hò* means "good."

Hello everyone - dăi gei hò
- *Dăi gei* means "everyone."
- Use this to greet multiple people, like when you are in a group setting.

How are you? - lì hò bó?
- Adding *bó* to the end of a sentence makes the phrase a question.

__ good morning - __, zà
- *Zà* means "early," but when combined with a name in front, it is a friendly way to greet friends and family in the morning.
- Fill in the blank with a name or person.
- For example, "good morning, grandmother" would be "ah mà, zà."

Have you eaten? - jiăk° bà beh?
- *Jiăk°* means "to eat," *bà* means "full" and *beh* is added to a sentence to ask if an action has been done yet.
- Many people will greet others with *jiăk° bà beh* to ask if they have eaten or not. Don't feel like you need to use this, but don't be surprised if someone greets you like this.
- To respond, you can say *wà ăh bĕh jiàk°* which means "I have not eaten yet." The tone for *jiàk°* changes because of tone sandhi.
- You can also say *wà jiăk° bà liào* which means that you have already eaten until you are full.

lì hò!

I'm happy to see you - wà jin hua-N hèe kuà-N diŏh° lì
- *Jin* means "really" and *hua-N hèe* (notice the nasal sound mark) means "happy."
- *Kuà-N* means "to see" and *diŏh°* indicates the tense of the verb "to see."
- *Lì* means "you."

Long time no see - jin gù bŏ kuà-N diŏh° lì
- *Jin gù* means "it's been a long time" and *bŏ* means "have not."

Thank you - gám sia

You're welcome - bián kèi° kĭ

WHERE ARE YOU FROM?

To ask someone what country they are from, we say *lì sǐ tòh lòh láng?* We already know that *lì sǐ* means "you are," but what does *tòh lòh láng* mean? *Tòh lòh* means "where" and *láng* means "person" or "people."

To respond, say *wà sǐ ___ láng.* Fill in the blank with the country you are from! Look to the next page for the names of some countries in Hokkien. Remember, you can also say *náng* instead of *láng.*

lì náng sǐ tòh lòh láng?
(what country are y'all from?)

wà sǐ sin-ka-po láng!
(i am singaporean!)

wà sǐ bí kòk° láng!
(i am american!)

9

COUNTRIES

Sin-ga-pō

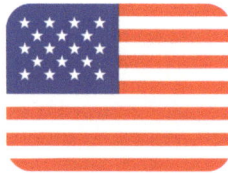

Bí kŏk°

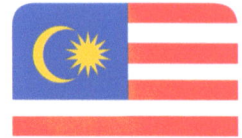

Jiu hù

Ìn-dor

Tiong-kŏk°

Hui-lŭt°-bīn

Ka-na-dái

Jĭt°-pùn

Tài-kŏk°

Ying-kŏk°

Huàt kŏk°

Tăi-wān

HOW OLD ARE YOU?

Now we will learn how to ask how old someone is, and how to say your age, or the age of objects like cars, houses, etc.

How old are you - lì guí huĕh?
- *Guí huĕh* means "how old" in Hokkien.

I am __ years old - wà __ huĕh
- Fill in the blank with how old you are.
- For example, *wà sa huĕh* would mean "I am three years old."

How old is he/she - yi guí huĕh?
- This is the same question as "how old are you" but the pronoun is switched to *yi* to say "he" or "she."

He/she is __ years old - yi __ huĕh
- Again, simply fill in the blank with how old the person is.

How old is this __ - zìt˚ ĕh __ guī ní?
- To ask the age of objects, like cars, we use a different question.
- *Zìt° ĕh* means "this" and *guī ní* means "how many years."
- Fill in the blank with the age of the object.

This __ is __ years old - zìt˚ ĕh __ __ ní
- To respond to the previous question, fill in the first blank with the object you are talking about and the second blank with the age of the object.
- For example, *zìt° ĕh chiā làk° ní* would mean "this car is six years old."

lì guí huĕh?
(how old are you?)

11

BASIC CONCEPTS

In this chapter, we will learn some basic concepts that will help you understand and speak Hokkien more fluently.

IS/ARE

There are many different words for the various forms of the words "is" and "are" in Hokkien, and they each serve different purposes. The first, *si*, is used to link equivalent things. See the examples below.

This is my dog - zìt° sǐ wà ěh gào
- *Zìt°* is a short form to mean "this." The tone on *si* changes to *sǐ* because of tone sandhi.
- *Wà ěh gào* means "my dog."

My name is - wà ěh miá sǐ
- We know this phrase from before, but to reiterate, this means "my name is."

He is my friend - yi sǐ wà ěh pěng yìu
- *Yi* means "he/she" and *sǐ* here means "is."
- *Wà ěh pěng yìu* means "my friend."

The next word used for "is" is *jin*. This is used for describing things like emotions, appearances, temperature, and even taste! Let's look at a few examples.

This soup is very delicious - zìt° ěh tēng jin hó jiàk°
- *Zìt° ěh* means "this" and *tēng* (pronounced almost like "tounge") means soup.
- *Jin* technically means "really" but it acts as the word "is" in this sentence.

She is very beautiful - yi jin suì
- *Yi* means "he" or "she."
- *Jin* means "really" but again acts as the word "is."
- *Suì* means "beautiful."

Finally, the word for "are" is *wǔ*. In some cases, this means "there are." But, it can also mean "to have." Let's look at examples of when to use *wǔ*.

There are two people - wǔ ňng ěh láng
- Here, *wǔ* is used to mean "there are."
- Instead of using *li* for "two," we use *ňng* because we are counting things (people).

I have a dog - wà wǔ jǐt° jià gào
- Here, *wǔ* means "to have." Use context to identify which meaning of *wǔ* is being used.
- *Jǐt° jià gào* means "a dog."

-ING

To put the word "is" before a verb and add –ing to the end of a verb, we say *lēh*. Here are some examples.

What are you doing - lì lēh zò sìh˚ mìh˚?
- The word *lēh* is the word makes the "-ing" here.
- *Zò* means "doing" and *sìh˚ mìh˚* means "what."

He is eating - yi lēh jiàk˚
- *Lēh* is again used to create the "-ing."

AT

The word for "at" is *dǐ*. Let's look at some examples.

He is at home - yi dǐ cǔ
- *Dǐ* means "at" and indicates location in this sentence.
- *Cǔ* means "home" in Hokkien.

I am at the market - wà dǐ pā sàt˚
- *Pā sàt˚* means "market" in Bahasa Melayu and is adopted for use in Singaporean Hokkien.

We are at school - wà náng dǐ ǒh˚ dńg
- Again, *dǐ* indicates location and acts as the word "at."
- *Ǒh˚ dńg* means "school" in Hokkien.

pā sàt˚ - market

ǒh˚ dńg - school

cǔ - home

THIS/THAT

To say "this" in Hokkien, we say *zìt° ěh*. To say "that" in Hokkien, we say *hìt° ěh*. But, sometimes we do not use the *ěh* after the *zìt°* or *hìt°*. It depends on the sentence. If we want to say "this is" or "that is" we say *zìt° sǐ* or *hìt° sǐ*. But, if we want to say "this object is" or "that (object) is" we use the format of *zìt° ěh* and *hìt° ěh*.

This soup is spicy - zìt˚ ěh tēng jin hiǎm
- Here, we use the *ěh* because we are describing an object/noun.
- *Hiǎm* means "spicy."

That is my younger brother - hìt˚ sǐ wà ěh siō di
- Here, we are using *hìt° sǐ* because we are saying that something (in this case someone) is my younger brother.
- *Siō di* means "younger brother."

siō di **- younger brother**

POSSESSIVE

Possession in Hokkien is very similar to possession in Mandarin. To indicate possession, follow this formula.

pronoun + ěh + object

My dog - wà ěh gào
- *Wà ěh* means "mine" or "my" and *gào* means "dog."

Your cat - lì ěh niǎo
- Same thing here, *lì ěh* means "your" and *niǎo* means "cat."

gào **- dog**

niǎo **- cat**

His bike - yi ěh kah-dǎh-chiā
- *Yi ěh* means "his" or "hers" and *kah-dǎh-chiā* means "bicycle."

Our friend - wà náng ěh pěing yìu
- *Wà náng ěh* means "ours" or "our" and *pěing yìu* means "friend."

Y'all's clothes - lì náng ěh sā-N
- *Lì náng ěh* means "y'all's" or "you guys'" and *sā-N* means "clothes."

Their ball - yi náng ěh gíu
- *Yi náng ěh* means "their" and *gíu* means ball.

kah-dǎh-chiā
- bicycle

5WS & 1H

The five Ws and one H are as follows:

- Who - *siáng*
- What - *sìh° mìh°*
- Where - *dòh° lòh°*
- When - *dǐ sí*
- Why - *àn zuà*
- How - *àn zuà + verb* - when asking "how to + verb"
- How - *luǎ gù* - when asking "how long"
- How - *luǎ zueh* - when asking "how much"
- How - *guí ěh* - when asking "how many"

bǔn dái **- questions**

Who ate my noodles - siáng jiǎk° wán wà ěh mee?
- *Siáng* means "who" and *jiǎk° wán* means "finished eating."
- *Wà ěh mee* means "my noodles."

What is your name - lì giò sìh° mìh° miá?
- We know this phrase already. The words *sìh° mìh°* act as the word "what."

mee **- noodles**

Where is my cell phone - wà ěh cíu gī dǐ dòh° lòh°?
- *Cíu gī* means "cell phone" in Hokkien.
- Since we are asking about location, we use *dǐ* to say "is."
- Finally, we put *dòh° lòh°* to ask "where."

When can I go to the market - wà dǐ sí ěh sái kì pā sàt°?
- *Dǐ sí* means "when" and *ěh sái* means "can."
- *Kí* means "to go."

See the next page for more examples.

cíu gī **- cell phone**

Why can't you come to my house - lì àn zuà buěh sái lái wà ěh cǔ?
- *Àn zuà* means "why" in this case.
- *Buěh sái* means "cannot" and *lái* means "to come."
- *Wà ěh cǔ* means "my house" or "my home."

How do I walk to school - wà àn zuà giǎ-N kì ǒh° dńg?
- *Àn zuà* here means "how" and *giǎ–N* means "to walk."
- *Kì ǒh° dńg* means "to go to school."

How long does it take for me to walk to school - wà giǎ-N kì ǒh˚ dńg su yào luǎ gù?
- This sentence directly translated means "I walk to school need how long?"
- *Giǎ–N* means "to walk" and *kì ǒh° dńg* means "go to school."
- *Su yào* means "need" and *luǎ gù* means "how long."

How many people are there - wǔ guí ěh láng?
- *Wǔ* means "there are" and *guí ěh* means "how many."
- *Láng* means "people." Sometimes people say *náng* instead. Both are correct.

CONJUNCTIONS

The following are the most common conjunctions used in Hokkien.

- If – *nǎ sǐ*
- Or – *ǎh sǐ*
- Also – *mǎ sǐ*
- But – *dǎn sǐ*
- And – *gǎh*
- Because – *yin wěe*
- So – *sór yǐ*

png - rice

kiòh˚ cǔ - to do housework

I am happy because you did housework - wà jin hua-N hèe yin wěe lì kiòh˚ cǔ
- *Jin hua–N hèe* means "very happy" and *yin wěe* means "because."
- *Kiòh° cǔ* means "to do housework."

Do you want to eat noodles or rice - lì ài jiǎk˚ mee ǎh sǐ png?
- *Ài* means "to want" and *mee* means "noodles."
- *Ǎh sǐ* means "or" and *png* means "rice."

I want noodles and rice - wà ài jiǎk˚ mee gǎh png
- Here we use *gǎh* which means "and." *Gǎh* can also mean "with." Pay attention to the context of the sentence to understand its meaning.

I LIKE/I WANT

In Hokkien, "I want" is *wà ài* and "I like" is *wà su kàh°*. Here are some example sentences.

He wants to eat durian - yi ài jiăk° liĕw lián
- The sentence structure here is the same as English.
- *Yi* means "he" or "she" and *liĕw lián* means durian.

liĕw lián -
durian

I like to eat durian - wà su kàh° jiăk° liĕw lián
- *Su kàh°* can also be used to say "love" even though it means "to like." For example, you could say *wà su kàh° lì* which means "I love you."

CAN/ABLE TO

In Hokkien we say *ĕh hiào* for expressing your ability to do something, like a skill. But *ĕh sài* is used when talking about if something is possible.

Can you help me - lì ĕh sài băng máng wà bó?
- Here, we use *ĕh sài* because we are asking if it is possible for someone to help.
- *Băng máng* means "to help" and *bó* indicates that this is a question.

Can you run - lì ĕh hiào zào bó?
- Here, we use *ĕh hiào* because we are asking about the ability of someone to run. Running is a skill.
- *Zào* means "to run."

bāng máng - to help

zào - to run

YES/NO

In Hokkien, no single word represents "yes" and no single word represents "no." When wanting to say "yes" or "no" to a question or demand, use the verb that is used by the person asking you the question. See the examples below.

Do you like bananas - lì su kàh˚ geing jiō bó?
- *Geing jiō* means "bananas."

Yes, I like them - diòh˚, wà su kàh˚
- *Diòh°* means "yes" in this case.
- For a positive response to the previous question, you can reply simply with *su kàh°*, indicating that you like bananas to shorten the response.
- As you can see, the verb "to like" or *su kàh°*, is repeated in the response.

No, I don't like them - wà bó su kàh˚
- Again, the verb is repeated.
- For the negative response, the negator *bó* acts as "no" and "don't."

For different sentences and questions, there are different affirmatives and negatives. For example:

I can't help you wash the car - wà buěh sài bāng máng lì suéh chiā
- *Buěh* is the negator for the verb "to be able to" or *ěh sài*.
- *Suéh chiā* means "to wash the car."

I do not know - wà mm zai
- Here *mm* is the negator for *zai* which means "to know."

Yes or no - sǐ mm si?
- *Sǐ* is the "yes" and *mm si* is the "no."

geing jiō - banana

suéh - to wash

su kàh˚/bó su kàh˚ - to like/dislike

18

COLORS

Put *sèk*, which means color, after any color. "Brown" is named after coffee, *kopi*, in Hokkien.

Black	White	Gray	Red
or sèk°	pěh sèk°	heh hu sèk°	ang sèk°

Orange	Yellow	Green	Blue
gam sèk°	ňg sèk°	tsee sèk°	lǎm sèk°

Purple	Pink	Brown	Gold
giǒ sèk°	tsuí-ǎng sèk°	kopi sèk°	gim sèk°

To describe objects with colors, place the color after the number and measure word, but before the noun.

number + measure word + color + ěh + noun

In Hokkien, measure words change depending on the object/thing being counted. Most languages are like this. In English we don't always use measure words ("a car") but sometimes we do, as when we say "a sheet of paper." Let's look at some examples to understand these concepts! We won't go over all the measure words, just a few.

A black car - jit jià or sèk° ěh chiā
- *Jit jià* is the number and measure word and means "a" or "one."
- *Or sèk°* means "black" and *ěh* is a word used to indicate possession.
- The word for "car" is *chiā*.

An orange shirt - jit nià gam sèk° ěh sā-N
- *Jit nià* is the number and measure word and means "a" or "one." For clothing, *nià* is used as the measure word.
- *gam sèk°* means "orange" and *ěh* indicates possession.
- The word for "shirt" is sā-N.

A brown dog - jit jià kopi sèk° ěh gào
- *Jit jià* is the number and measure word and means "a" or "one."
- *Kopi sèk°* means "brown" and *ěh* once again indicates possession.
- The word for "dog" is *gào*.

CONVERSATION TOPICS

FAMILY

Talking about your family is very important. Here are some of the most common words used to talk about family, and some phrases that can help the conversation flow.

FAMILY MEMBERS

English	Hokkien
Father	Lăo pĕh
Mother	Lăo bù
Wife	Bòr
Husband	Āng
Children	Géen nà
Son	Da bor già-N
Daughter	Za bór già-N
Grandchildren	Sōon
Grandaughter	Za bór sōon
Grandson	Da bor sōon
Elder brother	Duă hiā-N
Younger brother	Sió di
Elder sister	Duă jì
Younger sister	Sió beh
Woman	Za bòr
Man	Da bōr
Maternal grandma	Guă-mà
Maternal grandpa	Guă-gōng
Paternal grandma	Ah-mà
Paternal grandpa	Ah-gōng

PHRASES ABOUT FAMILY

I have a ___ - *wà wŭ jĭt˚ ěh* ___
- *Wà wŭ* means "I have" in Hokkien.
- *Jĭt˚ ěh* means "one" or "a."
- Fill in the blank with a family member. For example, *wà wŭ jĭt˚ ěh sío di* which means "I have a younger brother."

This is my ___ - *zìt˚ sĭ wà ěh* ___
- *Zìt˚ sĭ* means "this is" and *wà ěh* means "my."
- Fill in the blank with a family member. For example, *zìt˚ sĭ wà ěh guă–gōng* which means "this is my maternal grandfather."

That girl is my ___ - *hìt˚ ěh za bòr sĭ wà ěh* ___
- *Hìt˚ ěh* means "that" and *za bòr* means "girl."
- You can replace the *za bòr* with *da bōr* when talking about a boy.
- Again, fill in the blank with a family member.

I have ___ ___ - *wà wŭ ___ ěh* ___
- Fill in the first blank with the number of a certain family member you have.
- Fill in the second blank with the family member you are talking about.
- For example, *wa wŭ sa ěh duă jì* which means "I have three older sisters."

gēi láng - **family**

WORK

This section is similar to the last section. These phrases and words will help you talk about work and school.

JOBS

English	Hokkien
Doctor	Ló goōn
Lawyer	Lŭt° sū
Student	Hăk° seīng
Teacher	Lăo sū or sian sī
Nurse	Missy
Policeman	Ma tá
Banker	Gin hăng kā

PHRASES ABOUT WORK

Where do you work - lì dĭ dòh˚ lòh˚ zò gāng?
- *Zò gāng* means "work."
- *Dĭ dòh° lòh°* means "where."

I work at ___ - wà dĭ ___ zò gāng
- Fill in the blank with where you work.
- For example, *wà dĭ or-pìc zò gāng* means "I work at the office." *Or-pìc* means "office."
- You could also say *wà dĭ gin hăng zò gāng* which means "I work at the bank." *Gin hăng* means "bank."

Where do you study - lì dĭ dòh˚ lòh˚ tăk˚ tsĕk˚?
- *Tăk° tsĕk°* means "to study."

I am a university student - wà si dai hak seing
- *Dai hăk° seīng* means "university student."

**ma tá -
policeman**

22

FEELINGS

This section is about expressing feelings and emotions. These phrases and words will help you talk about how you feel.

I feel ___ - wà jin ___
- *Jin*, as you may remember, means "really."
- So, *wà jin* means "I'm really" and can be used to express feelings and emotions.
- Fill in the blank with whatever feeling/emotion you want to say. For example, *wà jin hua-N hèe* means "I am happy."

FEELINGS

English	Hokkien
Happy	Hua-N hèe
Stressed	Àp° làt°
Afraid	Giã-N
Angry	Gĭn sín or kí hōng
Tired	Sien
Excited	Chi kĕk°
Busy	Bo éng
Embarrassed	Pái sei

TIME

TELLING TIME

The formula for telling time in Hokkien is pretty straightfoward.

zìt° zun sĭ+ hour digit +diám + minute digit + hōon

Look below for examples using this formula, as well as how to ask for the time.

What time is it - zìt° zun guí diàm?
- *Zìt° zun* means "right now" and *guí diàm* means "what time."

It is 3:25 - zìt° zun sĭ sa diám lĭ zăp° gŏr hōon
- As you can see, we simply put the hour digit and the minute digit into the formula to tell the time.
- The hour digit here is *sa* or "three" and the minute digit is *lĭ zăp° gŏr* or "twenty five" in English.

It is 12:10 - zìt° zun sĭ zăp° lĭ diám zăp° hōon
- Again, we add the hour and minute digits to the formula to say the time.

DAYS OF THE WEEK

English	Hokkien
Monday	Bài yĭt°
Tuesday	Bài li
Wednesday	Bài sā
Thursday	Bài sĭ
Friday	Bài gor
Saturday	Bài làk°
Sunday	Léh bǎi

HELPFUL PHRASES

It is useful to know the following phrases when talking about the days of the week:

Today is Monday - geen lìt˚ sǐ bài yǐt˚
- *Geen lìt˚* means "today" and *sǐ* means "is."
- *Bài yǐt˚* means "Monday," but you can replace it with any day of the week to say what day it is.

Yesterday was Monday - zá lìt˚ sǐ bài yǐt˚
- *Zá lìt˚* means "yesterday."
- Again, you can replace the words for "Monday" with any day of the week.

Tomorrow is Monday - miá lìt˚ sǐ bài yǐt˚
- *Miá lìt˚* means "tomorrow."
- Again, you can replace the word for "Monday" with any day of the week.

MONTHS/YEARS/DATE

To say the date, we must first learn the months in Hokkien. See the table below for how to say the months.

English	Hokkien
January	Yìt° guèh°
February	Lǐ guèh°
March	Sa guèh°
April	Sì guèh°
May	Gǒr guèh°
June	Lǎk° guèh°
July	Cìt° guèh°
August	Poèh° guèh°
September	Gáo guèh°
October	Zǎp° guèh°
November	Zǎp° yìt° guèh°
December	Zǎp° lǐ guèh°

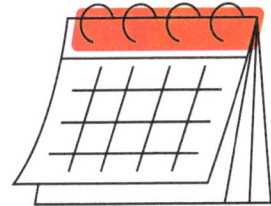

As you can see, the months are simply the number of the month is plus the word *guèh*.

Look to the next page to learn how to say the years in Hokkien, as well as how to ask for the date and say the date.

SAYING THE YEARS

To say the years in Hokkien, add the word ní to the year it is. For example:

1972 - yìt° gáo cìt° lĭ ní
- Just read out the single digits in order and add *ní*.
- In this case, "one, nine, seven, two" becomes *yìt° gáo cìt° lĭ*. Add *ní* and you are done!

2023 - lĭ kòng lĭ sa ní
- The same thing as before, just read out the single digits in order and add *ní*.

DATE

Great! Now that you know the months and the years, let's move on to dates.

What is the date today - geen lìt° guī ho?
- We know that *geen lìt°* means "today."
- *Guī ho* means "what number."

The formula for saying the dates is quite simple:

day of the week + year + ní + month + guèh + day + ho

Wednesday, July 19, 2023 - bài sã lĭ kòng lĭ sa ní cìt° guèh° zăp° gáo ho
- Simply put the day of the week, year, month, and day into the formula and you can say the date!

Today is Wednesday, July 19, 2023 - geen lìt° sĭ bài sã lĭ kòng lĭ sa ní cìt° guèh° zăp° gáo ho
- To be more direct and specific, you can say "today is" or *geen lìt° sĭ* before saying the date.

geen lìt° guī ho?
(what is the date?)

geen lìt° sĭ...
(today is...)

HAWKER CENTER STOP

Food is a huge part of Singaporean culture. This chapter goes over how to order food, drinks, and deal with money in Hokkien! Maybe next time you go to a hawker center, you can order in Hokkien!

ORDERING FOOD

Here are some useful phrases and words for ordering food in Hokkien:

What would you like to eat - lì ài jiǎk˚ sìh˚ mìh˚?
- *Ài jiǎk°* means "want to eat" and *sìh° mìh°* means "what."

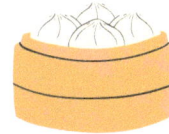

Do you want spice - lì ài mài hiām?
- *Ài mài* essentially is asking "want or don't want." Here, the negator for the verb *ài* or "to want" is the *m* before the second *ài*. Combined, the *m* and *ài* make *mài* which means "don't want."
- *Hiām* means "chili" or "spice."

What type of noodles do you want - lì ài jiǎk˚ sìh˚ mìh˚ kuàn mee?
- *Kuàn* means "kind" or "type" and *mee* means "noodles."

Do you want dry or soup noodles - lì ai dã mee ǎh sǐ mee tēng?
- *Dã mee* means "dry noodles" and *mee tēng* means "noodle soup."
- Take note of the *ǎh sǐ* which means "or."

Can I order ___ - wà ěh sài diám ___ bó?
- Fill in the blank with the dish you would like to order.
- *Wà ěh sài* means "can I" and *diám* means "to order," and *bó* indicates that you are asking a question.

I want to order ___ - wà ài diám ___
- *Wà ài* means "I want."
- Again, fill in the blank after the word "order" or *diám* with the dish you want.

One bowl of noodles - jǐt˚ wuá mee
- You can also order directly, and simply state what you want in terms of a bowl (wuá) or a plate (buá).
- Here, *jǐt°* means "one" and *mee* means "noodles."

I want/don't want chili - ài/mài hiām
- *Ài* means "want" and *mài* means "don't want."
- *Hiām* means "chili."
- You can replace the word for chili with another seasoning (vinegar, sauce, etc.)

For here or take away - jìt° dao jiàk° ăh sǐ dá bāo?
- This sentence more closely means "eating here or taking away."
- *Jìt° dao jiàk°* means "eating here" and *dá bāo* means "pack."

FOOD

English	Hokkien
Cooked rice	Png
Porridge (congee)	Béh
Noodles	Mee
Meat (add to the end of an animal, ex. gú băh° means cow meat)	Băh°
Cow	Gú
Pig	Dir
Chicken	Guēh
Duck	Ăh°
Egg	Nng
Fish	Hír
Tofu	Dau-hŭ

FRUITS & VEGETABLES

English	Hokkien
Banana	Geing jīo
Coconut	Yă chì
Lychee	Năi chī
Durian	Liěw lián
Ginger	Giū-N
Tomato	Ăng mŏh gío
Potato	Kan dăng
Vegetable	Căi

SEASONINGS

English	Hokkien
Salt	Yúm
Sauce	Zŭp°
Vinegar	Cŏr
Chili	Hiam jiō
Sugar	Téng

UTENSILS & CROCKERY

English	Hokkien
Spoon	Tng sí
Fork	Ciàm
Chopsticks	Dir
Bowl	Wuà
Plate	Puá

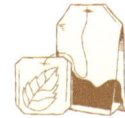

DRINKS

English	Hokkien
Water/Hot water	Zuì/sio zuì
A glass of water	Jĭt° pueh zuì
Coffee/Black coffee	Kopi/kopi or
Milk	Gŭ nī
Tea	Téh
Alcohol	Jiù
A bottle of beer	Jĭt° guăn pĕk° bìt°

MONEY

Let's learn how to say how much things cost and how to ask how much something costs in Hokkien.

How much - gui lui?
- This is how you ask for the price.
- *Gui* means "how much" or "how many" and *lui* means "money."

Dollar - kor

Cents - jiam

10-cents - găk°
- For example, 30 cents would be *sa găk°*.

$6.03 - lăk° kor sa jiam
- Simply put the number of dollars before *kor* and put the number of cents before *jiam*.
- Use *jiam* when the number of cents is under 10.

$18.30 - zăp poèh° kor sa găk°
- Simply put the number of dollars before *kor* and the number of "ten cents" before the *găk°*.

GETTING AROUND

In this chapter, you will learn how to say various vehicles as well as useful phrases and vocabulary for directions.

VEHICLES

Here are some common modes of transportation in Hokkien.

English	Hokkien
Car	Chiā
Bus	Gong chiā
Train	Hueh chiā
Plane	Bueh gī
Taxi	Taxi

chiā - car   **hueh chiā - train**   **bueh gī - plane**

DIRECTIONS

These are some useful phrases and vocabulary words for getting directions in Hokkien.

Where are you - lì dǐ dòh˚ lòh˚?
- Again, *dǐ* means "are" and indicates that we are asking about a location.

I am ___ - wà dǐ ___
- Fill in the blank with a location.

Where is ___ - ___ dǐ dòh˚ lòh˚?
- Fill in the blank with the place you are asking about.

How do I walk to ___ - kì ___ àn zuà gía-N?
- Fill in the blank with the place you are asking for directions to.
- Here, *àn zuà* means "how."

Walk straight - dĭt° dĭt° giá-N
- *Giá-N* means "to walk" and *dĭt° dìt°* means "straight."

To say where you are, you can also use the formula:

wà dĭ + place + ĕh + position

I am to the right of the park - wà dĭ gong hńg ĕh zià-N cìu béng
- *Gong hńg* means "park" and *zià-N cìu béng* means "right hand side."

DIRECTIONS VOCABULARY

English	Hokkien
Here	Zìt° dāo
There	Hìt° dāo
Nearby	Hù goon
Bus stop	Chiā zum
Left side	Dò cìu béng
Right side	Zià-N cìu béng
In front	Tăo zéng
Behind	Aŏ buèh
Road	Béh chia lor
Traffic light	Ăng tsee-N hèh
Restaurant	Caan guàn
Coffee Shop/stand	Kopi diăm
School	Ŏh° dńg
Park	Gong hńg
Hospital	Ló goon cǔ
To go/return home	Dńg cǔ
Turn (left or right)	Wān

HEALTH

PARTS OF THE BODY

English	Hokkien
Head	Táo
Eye	Băk° jīu
Nose	Pĭ-N
Ear	Hee-N
Mouth	Cuĭ
Teeth	Cuì kì
Neck	Ărm pòon
Throat	Nă áo
Hand	Cìu
Arm	Cíu bă
Foot	Kā
Leg	Kā
Stomach	Pàtt° tòr

MEDICAL PHRASES

These are some useful phrases and vocabulary words for talking about your health in Hokkien!

What part of your body hurts - lì ĕh seing kū dòh° lòh° tiă-N?
- *Seing kū* means "body" and *tiă-N* means "hurts."

My __ hurts - wà ĕh __ tiă-N
- Fill in the blank with a part of the body.
- *Wà ĕh* means "my" or "mine."

Does it hurt here - zìt° dāo ĕh tiă-N bó?
- *Zìt° dāo* means "here" and *bó* indicates that this is a question.

You need to take medicine - lì su yào jiǎk° yòh°
- *Jiǎk° yòh°* literally means "eat medicine" but can be used to say "take medicine."

My leg is bleeding - wà ěh kā lǎo huǐh°
- *Kā* means "leg."
- *Lǎo huǐh°* means "bleeding."

Can you help me - lì ěh sài bāng máng wà bó?
- Remember, we use *ěh sài* here because we are asking about the possibility of someone helping, not a the ability of someone to preform a certain skill.
- *Bāng máng* means "to help."

AILMENTS

English	Hokkien
Fever	Huàt° siō
Flu	Gám mor
Runny nose	Lǎo pǐ-N zuì
Cough	Ga sǎo
Itchy	Jiu-N
Bleeding	Lǎo huǐh°
Swollen	Zèng
Take medicine	Jiǎk° yòh°
Headache	Táo tiǎ-N
Sore throat	Nǎ áo tiǎ-N
Stomach ache	Pàtt° tòr tiǎ-N

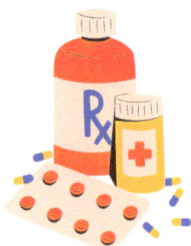

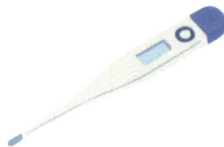

yòh° - **medicine**   huàt° siō - **fever**   ga sǎo - **cough**

34

USEFUL VOCABULARY

These are some common verbs, adjectives, and nouns that may help you continue your studying of Hokkien! These may have been repeated in this text already, but it is helpful to have them all in one spot.

VERBS

English	Hokkien
To see	Kuǎ-N
To listen	Tiā-N
To walk	Giá-N
To run	Zào
To go	Kǐ
To come	Lái
To use	Eng
To do	Zǒ
To buy	Buèh
To teach	Gǎ
To work	Zò gang
To garden	Zèng huēh
To wash	Suèh
To cook	Zír jiàk°

ADJECTIVES

English	Hokkien
Beautiful	Suì
Handsome	Yăn dáo
Big	Dua
Small	Suěh
Fast	Gèen
Slow	Ban
Early	Zà
Late	Wuă-N
Cheap	Pī-N
Expensive	Guǐ

NOUNS

English	Hokkien
Cell phone	Cíu gī
Cell phone number	Cíu gī hǒ bèh
Toilet/Bathroom	Cèh sòr
"Things"	Mǐng gia-N
Ball	Gíu

ACKNOWLEDGMENTS

This book would not have been possible without my wonderful Hokkien teacher, Eugene Lee, who has guided me from the very beginning of my journey with Singaporean Hokkien. The romanization system I used in this book was in large part based on a system he devised and which I later modified to make more intuitive for those who are familiar with pinyin, but are primarily English speakers. Eugene, thank you for your endless patience and guidance, as well as your thoughtful editing and proofreading along the way; learning a language has never been so fun.

I would also like to thank my *Gong Gong*, Albert Ng, who is the best Hokkien speaker I know. It was such a privilege to have a native Hokkien speaker just one phone call away.

Finally, thank you to my family, especially my *lǎo bù* and my *lǎo pěh*, but even my *sió di*. You are the reason I am connected to my multilingual heritage. *Lǎo pěh*, *lǎo bù*, thank you also for the editing, proofing, and overall advice that made this book the best it could be.

www.ingramcontent.com/pod-product-compliance
Lightning Source LLC
LaVergne TN
LVHW072130070426
835513LV00002B/53

* 9 7 9 8 2 1 8 2 5 8 0 6 1 *